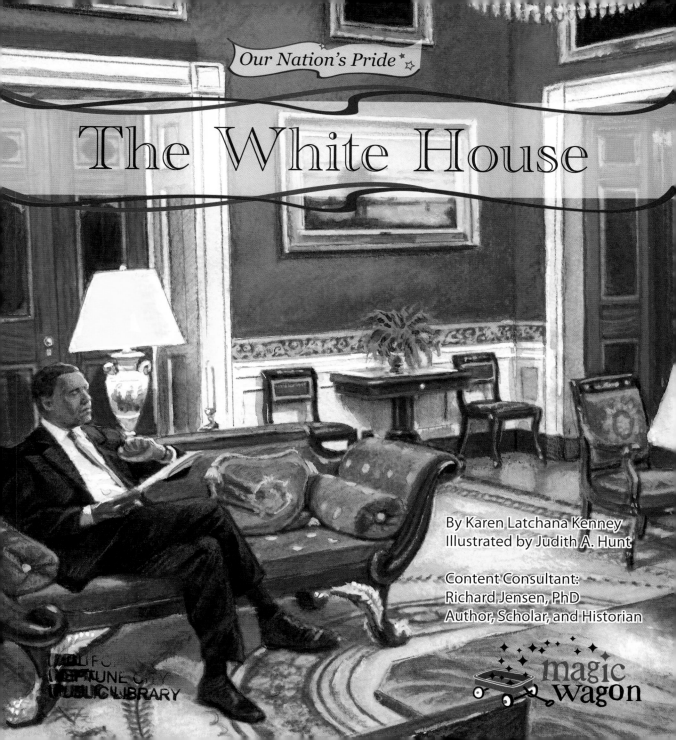

Our Nation's Pride

The White House

By Karen Latchana Kenney
Illustrated by Judith A. Hunt

Content Consultant:
Richard Jensen, PhD
Author, Scholar, and Historian

magic
Wagon

visit us at www.abdopublishing.com

Published by Magic Wagon, a division of the ABDO Group, 8000 West 78th Street, Edina, Minnesota, 55439. Copyright © 2011 by Abdo Consulting Group, Inc. International copyrights reserved in all countries. All rights reserved. No part of this book may be reproduced in any form without written permission from the publisher.

Looking Glass Library™ is a trademark and logo of Magic Wagon.

Printed in the United States of America, North Mankato, Minnesota.
092010
012011

 THIS BOOK CONTAINS AT LEAST 10% RECYCLED MATERIALS.

Text by Karen Latchana Kenney
Illustrations by Judith A. Hunt
Edited by Melissa Johnson
Interior layout and design by Becky Daum
Cover design by Becky Daum

Library of Congress Cataloging-in-Publication Data
Kenney, Karen Latchana.
  The White House / by Karen Latchana Kenney ; illustrated by Judith A. Hunt.
    p. cm. — (Our nation's pride)
  Includes index.
  ISBN 978-1-61641-154-1
  1. White House (Washington, D.C.)—Juvenile literature. 2. Washington (D.C.)—Buildings, structures, etc.—Juvenile literature. I. Hunt, Judith A., 1955- ill. II. Title.
  F204.W5K458 2011
  975.3—dc22
                                 2010014010

Table of Contents

A Famous Address

In Washington DC, visitors flock to 1600

Pennsylvania Avenue. On the street, they peer

through a tall, black fence. Across a huge lawn

stands a big, beautiful house. This is the White

House. The president of the United States lives

here.

By the Potomac River

In 1790, the United States was a brand-new nation. It needed a capital city. This was where the government buildings would stand side by side. The president would live in the capital, too.

President George Washington chose a spot by the Potomac River. The city was named *Washington* after the first president. DC stands for District of Columbia, the name of the area around the original city.

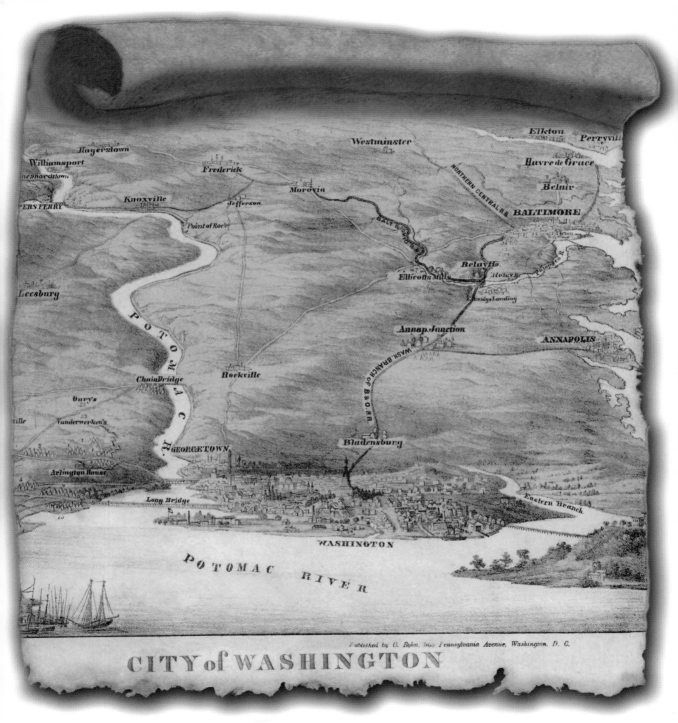

CITY of WASHINGTON

Published by C. Bohn, 565 Pennsylvania Avenue, Washington, D. C.

The Building Begins

On October 13, 1792, building began on the president's house. White-painted sandstone would form the outside walls. Workers from Scotland carved beautiful patterns into some of the stones. These framed the doors.

The work went slowly and carefully. Eight years later, the outside walls were finished.

8

A President Moves In

In 1800, the inside of the White House was still being built. The stairs and the rooms were not complete. It was cold and wet.

Even so, President John Adams and his wife, Abigail, moved in. Mrs. Adams hung their laundry to dry in the East Room. The house was not finished while the Adamses lived there. The next president, Thomas Jefferson, completed the building by 1809.

The War of 1812

Soon after the White House was finished, the United States and Great Britain were at war. They waged the War of 1812.

In August 1814, British soldiers marched into Washington DC. They set fire to the White House. Only the outside walls were left standing. Luckily, President James Madison's wife, Dolley, had many important items rescued. Among them was a famous painting of George Washington.

A New White House

By 1817, the White House was rebuilt. Over the years, it has been changed and made bigger. In 1902, the West Wing and the East Wing were added. Later, builders made both wings larger. Today, the White House has six floors and 132 rooms.

Naming the White House

The White House's sandstone walls are full of tiny holes. So, builders began sealing them with a special white paint in 1798. People started calling the building the "White House" for its color.

In 1901, President Theodore Roosevelt made "White House" the official name. Before that, the building was called the "Presidential Mansion," the "Presidential Palace," or the "Executive Mansion."

A Family Home

Today, the president's family lives on the

top two floors of the White House. This area has

kitchens, dining rooms, living rooms, bedrooms,

and bathrooms. It also has special rooms for music

and games. The White House even has tennis

courts, a swimming pool, a movie theater, and a

bowling alley!

The President at Work

The White House is not just a home. The president and his staff work there, too. The president's Oval Office is in the West Wing. He holds important meetings there. In the Press Room, reporters are busy. They gather news about meetings and other events at the White House.

Outside the West Wing is the beautiful Rose Garden. The president can walk along a path beside it.

Important Visitors

Some rooms in the White House are for hosting world leaders. In the Blue Room, important guests such as the queen of England can join the president and the First Lady. There, they can take in the view of the lawn. Later, they may enjoy a fancy dinner or a musical performance in the East Room.

An American Museum

The White House is like a museum. Famous paintings hang on the walls. Portraits of presidents and first ladies are also on view. Beautiful furniture and other objects fill every room. Many were gifts to the presidents. Others were bought by the leaders themselves.

What the White House Means

The White House is a symbol of the president. It is also a symbol of the United States. Presidents have signed laws here. They have given speeches and led the country through wars and disasters.

No other home of a world leader is free and open to the public. The White House is special because anybody can visit and see history happening.

Visiting the White House

You can visit the White House with a group. However, you must arrange a tour beforehand.

Walk through the rooms with your group. You will see artwork, antique furniture, and beautiful carpets and draperies. There have been weddings and performances in these rooms. World leaders have visited. Millions of Americans have toured here before you. This beautiful building belongs to the entire nation.

Fun Facts

- It takes 570 buckets of paint to cover the outside of the White House.

- The White House has 412 doors and 127 windows.

- President James Monroe's daughter was the first person to be married in the White House, in 1820. President Grover Cleveland was the only president to have his wedding in the White House, in 1886.

- Grover Cleveland's wife, Frances, was the only First Lady to have a baby in the White House.

- Until the 1860s, the White House was the largest house in the whole country.

- The White House has five chefs who can make dinner for 150 guests or snacks for 1,000.

Glossary

antique—an old item that has collectible value.

mansion—a big and grand house.

portrait—a painting or a picture of a person, usually of their face.

Press Room—the White House room where reporters ask the president questions.

reporters—people who find and report news for radio, television, newspapers, magazines, or other media.

sandstone—rock that is made of sand cemented together by clay, lime, or other materials.

symbol—something that stands for something else.

wing—a part of a building that comes out from the side of the main building.

31

On the Web

To learn more about the White House, visit ABDO Group online at **www.abdopublishing.com**. Web sites about the White House are featured on our Book Links page. These links are routinely monitored and updated to provide the most current information available.

Index